Only Then:
A Journey to Find Life's Greatest Gift

D. M. Cawley

ISBN: 9798652075170

DEDICATION

This book is dedicated to my soul mate, friend, and husband, Les. You are my guardian angel and love of my life.

To my sons, Chris and Chuck. You light up my life and make my heart smile!

To my daughters-in-law, Angela and Bridgette. Your love is reflected in the eyes of your daughters!

To my granddaughters, Alyssa, Grace, and Olivia. You are the reason for this book and my greatest joy

CONTENTS

In my feeble attempt to make some sense of this roller coaster called life, for years I have written. At first, for myself, then for others who asked me to put their feelings into words. It has given me great pleasure.

If through this book, others find comfort and answers, my cup is full and my heart grateful.

One of the greatest privileges of my lifetime has been my

my countless encounters with people who have chosen to

"bloom where they are planted."

The amazing souls that get up every morning facing insurmountable

obstacles yet never lose faith in their belief that life will get better.

Single moms and dads working two and three jobs trying to make

ends meet to provide a better life for their children.

Stepparents who walk into uncertainty with their hearts and

arms open wide.

Caregivers who start each day with a prayer on their lips

for strength.

The homeless, the broken, the addicted, those suffering

devastating loss or illness.

We see them every day, in every walk of life, these unsung

heroes.

Too many to mention yet they are all the same.

Amazing examples of hope, love, endurance and the capability

of embracing the proper perspective.

PERSPECTIVE

When my troubles seem insurmountable
and I feel I have been
given more than my share,
I simply look over my shoulder
to find humility waiting there.
The family living on the street
who would give anything to have a home,
The widow who aches for her husband's arms
Bravely facing life alone.
The parents who have experienced the death of a child
Find no comfort with no tears left to cry,
The person diagnosed with a terminal illness
so full of life, not ready to die.
The elderly living on a pittance
struggling each day to make ends meet,
The children who go to be hungry
awaken to find still nothing to eat.
Though we perceive our troubles insurmountable
Compared to others, they are minute from the start.
Happiness lies with the proper perspective
and can only survive in a grateful heart.

Life is so fleeting.

We foolishly think people we love and the joy we feel

will last forever.

Saying goodbye is never easy,

but it is magnified when someone we love

dies before they are gone.

ALZHEIMER'S

Why do we become so impatient
with the terminal and the old?
could it be memories of them healthy
have become more precious than gold?
Our minds know they have changed
and gently they are treated,
in our hearts they are still the same,
and so we feel deeply cheated.
It is an emotional roller coaster ride
when a loved one is not the same,
it is a devastation words can't express
when they, one day,
don't remember our name.
It is emotions we can't understand
and yet refuse to see,
it is a subconscious acknowledgment of,
"Oh, my God."
someday this could be me.
But mostly it's the realization
that no matter how much love and faith,
we still lack the power
to reset the hands of time.
What is lost will never come back.

The one thing we all search for is love.
The blessing of finding the "right person" is heaven sent,
but to love someone, lose them, then find love again,
that is magic.

ANNIVERSARY

If tomorrow God gave me another lifetime
I would choose to spend it with you,
The beginning of my completeness
was the moment we said, "I do."
I can't remember life before us,
my partner, lover and friend,
blessed with more than our share of happiness there
was never a heartache your smile couldn't mend.
In your arms I have felt a place of solitude,
in your eyes more love than I have ever known,
through the years our trials have made us stronger,
together we have grown.
Grown in our feelings and failings
focused on what is permanent,
in life, and what will pass,
my devotion is with you always,
except when you are a
pain in the ass!!

SECOND TIME

When I look in your eyes
I see something I thought I would never again see,
someone devoted to my happiness who takes
pleasure in caring for me.
God placed us in each other's lives
knowing we both needed a friend,
gone the stability of lifetime companions,
two hearts uncertain they would mend.
Our past has found a place in our hearts,
Precious memories for each of us to know,
our future built on tender love
and trust together we found the strength to let go.
Let go of what was and what might have been.
Only God knows the purpose for each life.
With a clear vision of tomorrow
and what together we have become,
we unite as husband and wife.
Our blessings are so many,
which only a few have found,
God's hand has truly touched our lives
the second time around.

A client's daughter was about to have a birthday and she asked me to write a poem for her.

My client had a rough childhood and was unable to express her feelings.

It gave me great pleasure to write......

SILENT LOVE

Raised by parents who believed in discipline
but found it difficult to show love
with words or a touch,
early on I developed a tough exterior
hoping then it wouldn't hurt so much.
Growing up my heartaches were many,
my moments of happiness few,
then God touched my life with a precious gift,
He blessed me with you.
Through the years I thanked Him
so many times for a child that means the world to me,
I gave you everything I could afford
except my vulnerable side to see.
I know I have hurt you
by words never said,
the guilt tears at my heart even now,
I want to tell you no parent could be more proud,
but words don't come easy
I was never taught how.

His smile lit up the room, his spirit lingered long after

he was gone.

He was my friend and coworker.

In the early 90's, AIDS was a death sentence.

One of my life's most treasured memories was being told

his family buried him with the original copy of . . . .

AIDS

I know there is a special place
where clouds are lined with love,
where hurt and pain no longer exist
and the sun shines bright above.
A place where no one feels the need to compete
or judge their fellow man,
a place where crystal oceans
hug the pure white sand.
I don't understand while knowing this
I still can't seem to let go,
I guess because you are such a part of my life
and I'm going to miss you so.
I only pray for the strength
to rejoice when you are called to that promised land,
a place where you will rest on God's shoulder
and He will hold you in His hand.

He was a gifted photographer by profession.

His passion was horses.

His family was his love and to our children he was Grandpa.

When he was diagnosed with throat cancer, he fought it

with the same zest he had for life.

He won the first battle but it returned with a vengeance....

DEATH OF A COWBOY

I can't blame you for not saying goodbye,
you did what you felt you must do,
my comfort lies with the knowledge
that the suffering is over for you.
We had so many beautiful years
and you knew we would always be there,
for your soul to find peace and comfort
is in my every prayer.
If there is a cowboy heaven,
forever you will ride up above,
I thank you for precious memories
you were so easy to love.
You must have known
you had a long ride ahead
and with time my heart will see,
you had your saddle bags
already.
Filled with dignity.

*Few things torture the heart more than saying goodbye
to our beloved pets.
We can't explain to them and the thought of losing that
unconditional love leaves a void in our hearts we never
forget.*

DECISION

Our minds know it is time, our hearts can't seem to let go,

the torment of making that decision is only for us to know.

The moment we give them their greatest peace is the

moment we lose our best friend,

we question whether we had the right

and when this hurt in our heart will end.

Our thoughts are of what we could have done if that cheek

were still here to kiss,

our memories consist of the times we weren't there and

all of the love we will miss.

Tomorrow will bring renewed strength with the realization

today wasn't goodbye,

precious friends and feelings are buried in our hearts and

there they never die.

A PRAYER FOR BUDDY

Please open your arms wide Saint Francis

for the sweetest of souls is on its way,

my grief is beyond comprehension

for we just said goodbye today.

Please reserve for him a special place

close to your tender care,

like me you will find when you need him,

without calling, he will know and be there.

You hold his happiness for eternity,

he captured my heart for years,

knowing he is in your loving animal heaven

gives me reason to smile through the tears.

I can't send you any pedigree papers

to reinforce in your eyes what he has been,

it is enough for me to know he is happy

and his legs will run once again.

With faith and a sense of humor

There isn't anything you can't do,

One will sustain you,

The other will see you through!!!

PMS

A couple of days out of the month
I can't believe I'm me,
a person I can't identify with
emerges for all to see.
I'm the woman impatiently glancing
at her watch while stopped at a traffic light,
convinced I'm surrounded by idiots
and only my opinion is right.
The people I smile at through clenched teeth,
the rest of the month I cherish and embrace,
how unstable I feel with this terrible urge
to slap them in the face.
I guess I have to admit it,
I'm a rebel without a cause,
and PMS merely child's play
compared to the mother lode
menopause.

HOUSEWORK

I take such pride in every facet of my life,

but with housework

there is something I lack,

I dream of the day I achieve immaculate

and search for the knack.

What do they mean check for dust in the corners?

My concern is the middle of the room,

bleach was made to make me sneeze

and the vacuum cleaner spells doom.

If I could do it just once

and have it stay that way,

maybe I could make some sense of this thing,

They have even named a season after it.

Why can't I associate with spring?

God bless each and every one of you

who find dust and look for more,

until I discover your secret satisfaction,

I will find solace in closing each door.

GRAVITY

It seems like such a dirty trick
for Mother Nature to play,
every part that used to be perky and cute
has somehow faded away.
You can imagine my shock
with wrinkles, gray hair,
and gone all I once held dear,
reality now smacks me in the face
each time I look in the mirror.
I don't mind the arthritis
or not always hearing when someone calls,
but boy do I wish I was quicker
when it comes to the trip and falls.
You can escape or fix just about everything
with a touchup, nip, or tuck,
But when it comes to gravity,
hold on to your hats.
I wish you lots of luck.

COOKING

When it comes to cooking

I'm not a gourmet

but I really stay on my toes,

my reply to my son,

when asked if the sausage was burned,

"You won't find any parasites in those."

TV dinners are unheard of in my league,

a box with an expiration date,

the only way they can be justified

is transferring the contents to a plate.

Pasta is really my specialty,

an opportunity for my guests to relax and dine,

the raves I receive are endless

as they open the third bottle of wine.

I guess I just have that special knack

for entertaining with a flare,

By the time I yell, "Come and get it,"

no one moves in awe.

They just stare.

It touches every family.

It breaks so many hearts.

Two people, too many obstacles, and too many words

spoken that can never be taken back or forgotten

DIVORCE

The severing of ties, the look in your eyes
as we face what we never thought would be.
The hurt, the denial, the heartache
of visualizing you without me.
The storybook love that captured our hearts,
the promise to be happy ever after.
The memory of our hearts beating as one
the sound of your laughter.
I tried to help you conquer your demons
putting our family in harm's way,
I made a promise to God to protect you
but a part of me dies every day.
The reality is I can't help you,
instead I must remain strong
for the one thing we did right,
little ears that heard too much,
as we destroyed our love,
must now be held extra tight.

*While watching the news one evening we saw a small boy
climbing a huge bank of snow to carry his little brother back
home.*

*His bravery, at this daunting task, brought tears to our eyes.
My husband looked at me and said, "I don't know why that
touched my heart enough to make me cry."*

EVEN MEN CRY

I don't know what makes me cry, it just wells up inside,

it's a feeling of vulnerability, emotions I can't hide.

It's the sight of a child carrying his brother over a bank

of snow,

or a dedication that lasts a lifetime, an accomplishment I

will never know.

It's the fellow man who never quits when the odds are he

will fail,

or the face of a soldier saluting our flag war-tired and pale.

It's the thousands who don't believe

they can make a difference

who will never understand,

or the person bridging race

and religion to help their fellow man.

I have been through the spectrum of emotions on one end

sorrow, the other end joy,

Why do I question the formation of a tear in my eye?

While discovering the man somewhere I lost the boy.

Childhood is such a special time for children

and parents alike.

The traditions of Santa, the Easter Bunny and Tooth Fairy

bring so much pleasure and joy.

There comes a time, we all dread, when our little ones start

to grow up and question this magical time in their lives.

IS THERE REALLY A SANTA

A part of my heart was breaking

a monumental task, I knew

someday it would happen

this question they would ask,

"Is there really a Santa?" with a slight tear in their eye,

the question I dreaded through their young years

that makes me want to cry.

To say there is no Santa

is to say December love doesn't exist,

the month we don't meet a stranger and rekindle the

friendships we have missed.

I say, my child there is a Santa.

He lives in each child's heart,

when you doubt he has a place in it,

that is when misgivings will start.

My child there is a Santa he lives in each child's prayer,

he is as real as your dreams and as long as you believe

in your heart he will always be there.

Yes, I still believe in Santa

and refuse to put those dreams on hold,

for believing is one of life's greatest treasures

and playing Santa more precious than gold.

Life is so precious and short.

When we lose a loved one our hearts think they will

never heal, our minds know they have found peace,

but the vulnerability and loss consume us.

It is then that our souls step in to carry us through.

GRIEF

A time when only a numb disbelief

helps alleviate the pain,

short durations of sleep end

with the reality that life won't be the same.

It is then that God steps in to carry us through tomorrow,

He provides precious memories to help ease our sorrow.

He holds us in His gentle hand until our eyes are dry,

He parts the clouds of our darkest hour

to illuminate the sky.

Take comfort in the love you brought to their lives

and a part of your heart they will always share,

forgive the awkwardness of friends

with insignificant words

and know they truly care.

The devastating ripples of mental illness far exceed those
of the sufferer.
Yet, the endless emotional struggles of family and friends
pale compared to the unthinkable price so many victims
of this debilitating disease pay.

ONCE AGAIN

Once again we wish that you were here

to see the joy in their eyes,

every milestone, every minute,

our minds cope, but a part of us dies.

Once again, we try to understand

why you felt you couldn't stay,

Your soul must have been so tortured

to not see another way.

Once again, we stay strong for each other

and hold on to the memory of your kiss,

each night crying into our pillows

you can't imagine how much you are missed.

Once again, we pick up the pieces

to a family and hearts broken in two,

Our greatest heartache?

The realization of the pain

you were going through.

One of the most painful lessons we learn is not everyone

we love will remain a part of our entire life's journey.

Relationships, friends, and the most difficult family members.

BROKEN

We keep using broken pieces
and expect them to fit,
words spoken, hearts broken,
years go by and yet
we refuse to quit.
You might bend me,
but you will never break me again
I'm not the person I was before,
I wish you well with every aspect of your life,
I simply won't do this anymore.
When looking back, on our time together,
I will be grateful for the time we had,
bittersweet, like life,
in my memory's eye
nothing is completely bad.
Tomorrow will bring a new beginning
and the start of a bright new day,
We must learn to love some people
from a distance
and our hearts need to know that's okay.

Few things in life tug at our heartstrings more than letting go

when it is time for our children to "leave the nest" for a

life of their own.

I find it odd that as long as I have written, when it comes

to my husband, sons, and grandchildren, I draw a blank.

Perhaps some feelings run so deep they are better left

in one's heart.

With the exception of......

A MOTHER'S PRAYER
FOR HER CHILDREN

Dear God,

Please wrap your protective arms around them

as when they were small I was able to do,

they need a much stronger and longer reach

that can only come from you.

Please guide them in the right direction

as they venture out on their own,

I find comfort knowing with you in their hearts

they will never be alone.

Please gather their guardian angels

to surround them each step of the way,

when they fall or fail

they will need them the most

so please ask them to stay.

Through encouraging their need to go out in the world

for precious room to grow,

I have found while loving is so easy

the courage is in letting go.

LEGACY OF LOVE

When will my heart stop breaking

each time I walk in the door?

When will my mind finally accept

you just won't be there anymore?

Perhaps not in body

but your spirit will always remain,

The love, the laughter, the memories

will always be the same.

Each time I see your kindness reflected

in the eyes of our son,

I will be reminded of your gentle spirit

and a life and race well run.

Your impact will live forever,

our broken hearts will slowly heal,

death can take the physical being,

the legacy of love it can never steal.

We know your journey here was completed

and God called you to His side,

forever grateful for the time we had,

in our hearts you never died.

My faith has and always will be my greatest source of strength

and comfort.

If I could give one gift to anyone in the world, it would be

the amazing feeling of knowing you are never alone.

Life can beat you up, people can let you down, and circumstances

can break your heart.

When I become disillusioned, there is always hope,

love and peace, and it is as close as a prayer.

SANDCASTLES

Dear God,

Whatever happened to the sandcastles

I built on the beach that day?

I suppose, as with the innocence of childhood,

waves of reality washed them away.

Whatever happened to trusting

and believing in all others say and do?

Did I replace caring with this barrier

when finding dreams don't always come true?

Whatever happened to my belief

in a world I thought I understood?

Why has it become so easy to acknowledge the bad

and dismiss so much of the good?

By far the hardest lesson I have learned

through life's hardships, heartaches and hassles,

treasure each moment and memory of innocence

and, yes,

sandcastles.

GOD'S ANSWER TO SANDCASTLES

My Child,

Your sandcastles still exist.

They are now simply one with the ocean.

They enable me to provide the beach

with the waves' gentle motion.

You stopped trusting and believing in others

the day you started to doubt yourself,

it isn't easy to trust and believe when betrayed

so you put your feelings on a shelf.

How tragic the day you started to believe

one person can't make a difference,

pushing aside the example I have shown

giving in to others insistence.

Though adversity may rest on your shoulders,

with faith in your heart,

uncertainty you can bear,

Use the strength of my love to better your world.

When you falter I'm as close as a prayer.

THE STRUGGLE

Dear God,

Challenges in life are seldom easy,

my faith has always seen my through,

the struggle is so real,

so little time and so much to do.

I'm so grateful for all of my blessings

and the strength you have given me,

so often hurting for the heartache of others

and the world that I see.

I have felt the sting of rejection,

choosing to wear my heart on my sleeve,

I don't understand why I haven't given up

steadfast in what I believe.

Perhaps in the end it is the struggle

where my true happiness lies,

for I would never want to live a life

unable to hear another soul when it cries.

GOD'S ANSWER TO THE STRUGGLE

My Child,

I never promised life would be easy,

I never said it would be fair,

when you face heartache and hardship,

I promised to always be there.

The blessings you are able to see,

are for some cloaked in disguise,

Only your faith has allowed you to see these gifts

through my loving eyes.

Having felt the sting of rejection

has given you compassion

to seek hurting souls,

and the strength to lift a broken world with the promise

of what the future holds.

I use my strongest soldiers in battle,

steadfast they will always remain,

for only those who have experienced the darkness

can understand the pain.

DEATH OF A CHILD:
A MOTHER'S PRAYER

Dear God,

You have given me my share of heartache,

but I knew you would always be there,

now broken, shattered, and bewildered

it is more than I can bear.

You said that you would carry me

when I couldn't stand on my own,

but this grief has such a hold on my heart

I feel so all alone.

You entrusted her to my gentle care

and I loved her for so long,

I carried her for nine months

and taught her right from wrong.

I have always accepted your decision

whether I felt it too strong or mild,

but no greater devastation can a mother endure

than the death of a child.

GOD'S ANSWER TO
DEATH OF A CHILD:
A MOTHER'S PRAYER

My Child,

You must know I will always love you,

I have promised to always be there,

your trials have not gone unnoticed,

trust in the power of each whispered prayer.

Each of your tears feels like a river

for my children's pain is also my own,

I will carry you through your darkest hours

you will never walk alone.

I entrusted her to your gentle care,

a strong and loving Mom to see her through,

I saw her future, I know your faith

that is why I placed her with you.

One day you will be reunited.

In the meantime, please understand,

no greater happiness could she have ever imagined

or held in a more gentle hand.

DEATH OF A CHILD: A FATHER'S PRAYER

Dear God,

When I heard I was going to be a father,

I asked for your guidance from above,

uneasy about being the best I could be,

you reassured me with your love.

Through the years I counted my blessings

and I always counted on you,

there wasn't a heartache I couldn't handle

for your love would see me through.

Today, you must have made a mistake,

God,

do you realize what you have done?

You took away my reason for living.

A man is not meant to outlive his son.

Words can't express the devastation that has rocked my
world

since the day you called him home,

I am surrounded by love and people who care.

Still my heart will live life alone.

GOD'S ANSWER TO
DEATH OF A CHILD:
A FATHER'S PRAYER

My Child,

Guidance was never needed from me.

You were the best of fathers from the start,

When I place a sweet soul for a short time on earth,

I place them with the kindest of hearts.

I place them in the gentlest of arms

only second to my own,

knowing love and contentment will fill their days

until I call them home.

Your child is resting with angels

and you will be reunited someday,

gather comfort from those around you

and peace from every prayer you pray.

I feel your pain, I walk by your side,

I send strength to all believers each one,

for I, too, have felt the devastation of loss

the day I gave the world my Son.

As I grow older, I have found I have tightened my circle, but my heart and arms will always remain open wide.

For we are all in this together.

We are all broken to some degree, searching for the greatest gift we can find in this life.

The ultimate treasure for our hearts . . .

Peace.

ONLY THEN

When you can embrace each moment

of this precious life and consider it just that,

when life's bases are loaded with two outs

and with optimism you grasp that bat.

When you can take time to understand an adversary

and in your heart make them a friend,

when you stop judging and realize you could be them

had you gone the places they have been.

When you can ache for a lifeless animal

or one lost without a home,

when the sight of a person hungry or homeless

cuts you to the bone.

When you can raise your eyes to heaven and

on bended knees solemnly pray,

when you believe when lost that neglected

someone above will always show you the way.

When every ounce of your being is filled with love

and for others your hand outstretched wide,

only then will you find the peace that had eluded you

for God's greatest gifts are found inside.

ACKNOWLEDGEMENTS

To Cindy - for your friendship and expertise in editing!

To Jean, Kathryn, Roseanne, Debbie, and Chuck - for all of your support and subtle reminders to get this book together!!

To Ray, Steve, and Lawrence - for your encouragement!

To Glenna and Angela - for your input getting this to the finish line!

To my nieces, Ronda and Kelli - your strength and courage inspires me!

To my hair family - you make every day a fun adventure!

FINAL THOUGHTS

If indeed, our lives resemble a roller coaster.
It is my hope that somewhere between our
highest highs and lowest lows we can all find
a place of contentment. A place where we can
hang our hats and know we are loved!